Best Evidence

Poems by Mark S. Osaki

Best Evidence: *Poems by Mark S. Osaki* /Mark S. Osaki. —2nd ed.

ISBN 979-8-2182-9897-5

For my mother, Haruye Murata Osaki

More Praise for Best Evidence

"Thoughtful, timely writing that demands further attention."

—Kirkus Review

"A well-done collection of poems seen from an Asian perspective of being an American. Interesting and enlightening."

—Goodreads

"Mark Osaki's mastery of language and his ability to elicit in his reader introspective thoughts/emotions is evident in his poetry. If you are looking to learn more about racial prejudice, war, and its resultant psychological aftereffects, this is definitely the book for you."

—Online Book Club

"Highly Recommended"

—Jenny Colvin
Librarian, Furman University
Podcaster, *Reading Envy*

"What a breath of fresh air! Mark tackles topics that other poets would never dare attempt. Within 55 pages, Mark paints images from which we have often turned our eyes away and stimulates emotions we most certainly buried deep within us. Best Evidence is not merely a compilation of life as seen through Asian eyes, but a work that can be seen through all eyes. Relatable, truthful and highly recommended!"

—Kristine Ohkubo,
Nickname Flower of Evil: The Abe Sada Story

"BEST EVIDENCE is a sparkling collection of lyrical an deftly-written poems. Its wide range means that there is something sure to appeal to the poetry lover in any reader. Osaki handles complicated family dynamics with the same dexterity as he approaches war and sex, masterfully describing the world in the way that only someone who has truly lived can."

—Christine-Marie Liwag Dixon
IndieReader

"Mark S. Osaki's BEST EVIDENCE goes beyond giving readers a sense of completion; it reaches into the past, present, and even an unseen future. It is for poetry lovers and humanitarians alike. It pulls at the heartstrings and makes the reader think more deeply about even the most mundane aspects of their own lives.

Osaki's work utilizes the same sort of deceptive simplicity found in the writing of such poets as William Carlos Williams. However, it is this very plainness which makes the poems accessible and more effective. Osaki uses straightforward language which lures readers into a seemingly-mundane, everyday conversation. Then, as the poem progresses, the rug gets pulled out from under the readers' feet with the introduction of an emotional or thematic twist that leaves them awestruck."

—US Book View

"I rate this book 4 out of 4 stars because of the fragile and transparent humanity that shines through these pages and for the unadorned but effective way to convey feelings and emotions. The clarity, both in style and content, of BEST EVIDENCE is so remarkable that anyone who reads it cannot fail to notice its lack of flaws. This is the true work of a master."

—On Bookshelves

"The book Best Evidence by Mark S. Osaki contains a fascinating collection of award-winning poetry. It's filled with poems that provide unique views on the issues of race, politics, war and many other topics that the average person usually doesn't talk about. That's what makes it such an unforgettable book."

—Azrevread Reviews

"A well-done collection of poems seen from an Asian perspective of being an American. An interesting and enlightening collection."

—Evilcyclist's Blog

"Mark Osaki's poems are among the most powerful, evocative and fearless I have encountered. His recent book, Best Evidence, is evidence of the talent, subtlety, power and creativity this extraordinary poet brings to his work. Osaki is a man who shows his vulnerabilities and wounds, yet plants them in gardens of grace, beauty and truth. Remarkable work. Be sure not to read it just once."

—Peter Damm
Author, *At the Water's Edge*

"It takes a lot of thinking to really appreciate or understand poems, but the words alone are lovely and deep that to ruminate every meaning is wonderful to do. Congrats to the author for his ability to express his thoughts and tell the story in a beautiful and creative way."

—A. Rickenbach
Author's Spotlight

"Poet Mark S. Osaki covers a number of poignant topics in Best Evidence. Each poem in the four sections gives you a glimpse of a formative moment in Osaki's life or expands your viewpoint on conflicts in the world. In each new work, Osaki captures powerful moments of longing and loss."

—Jennifer Reedo

BookJunkiez

"Evocative, deceptively straightforward and wry poetry that delivers a shock to the system."

—New York Quarterly Magazine

" Do you want a poetry book that will make you wonder about your life and that of every other person? Do you wish to read short poems that are written in the most basic form yet present you with epiphanies about what you call the norm? If the answer is yes, I recommend that you read this book."

—Francess Benhangag

Books Forum

Table of Contents

Acknowledgments

I am grateful to the National Endowment for the Arts for providing support to complete this book and would like to acknowledge the following publications in which some of the poems in this book originally appeared: *Atlantic Review, Báo Giấy, Beltway Quarterly, Berkeley Poetry Review, Birmingham Poetry Review, Breaking Silence: An Anthology of Contemporary Asian American Poets* (Greenfield Review Press), *California State Poetry Society, California Quarterly, Carrying the Darkness: The Poetry of the Vietnam War* (Texas Tech University Press), *The Chesapeake Reader, Clean Sheets, Contemporary Quarterly, Crosscurrents, Dark Tower, Drown in My Own Fears, Ergo, Fine Line, The Georgia Review, Hawaii Review,* Hiroshima Museum of Art, *Into the Teeth of the Wind, Journal of the American Academy of American Psychotherapists, The MacGuffin, Men of Our Time: Male Poetry in Contemporary America* (University of Georgia Press), *Message in a Bottle, New Orleans Poetry Review, Northern Contours, Phantasmagoria, The Poet's Haven, Rio Grande Review, San Fernando Poetry Journal, San Francisco Peace and Hope, South Carolina Review, Strath Poetry Journal* (Scotland), *Studies in Poetry, Third Wednesday, Three Rivers Poetry Journal, Windless Orchard, Wisconsin Review, Word Catalyst, Yellow Silk, Xanadu,* and *Zvezda.*

Walking Back the Cat

My Father Holding Squash

The photograph is several years old.
There in his garden my father dominates,
surrounded by his summer labor.

Still handsome in his sixties,
his tanned face radiates discipline
and good sense.

Though squatting, his legs are lean,
as if ready to spring. One is clearly
there by invitation.

Nothing is written across the photo,
but the caption is there all the same:
Look at this, you poetry-writing
jackass. Not everything I raise
is useless!

I look at the squash and smile
the wan smile of all beaten rivals,

noting the illiterate though eminently

bearable fruit

held proudly in his hands.

It's Relative

The stars seem magical for being so distant
yet we still find comfort in those nearest,
and even pretend to see in them familiar shapes
with recognizable names.

My two nieces are binary stars:
The farther is as indifferent as death,
the other close enough to warm me,
though I have remained as absent to both
as unread words upon a page.

Nothing but sun light or the promise of thaw
penetrates through the pull and rejection
of a family's gravity
or the void we unknowingly create.

Solitaire

Tonight each losing hand proved true
while I waited for some sign:
a ringing phone, a note slipped under my door,
or the sound of your car filling the empty street.

We are creatures given to random hope
when our aloneness closes in too suddenly,
swinging us off balance on the hinge
of some unnamable grief.

I once found a love letter, unaddressed, unsigned,
folded into the pages of a library book,
entombed like a message in a sealed bottle
that was never tossed from a sinking ship.

Perhaps the writer realized how unimportant
the choice of one's rescuer finally becomes,
like the accidental sense it makes
to invest too much on a single card

leaving everything to chance.

The Fish Heads

Their faces are flat profiles:
eyes frozen, glaring dumbly,
mouths gaping, stacked in rows
on powdered ice below the sign,
Huen's Grocery.
Why are they looking at us
that way, she asks. I smile,
tightly pulling her arm.
What do I know of any race
that should save it in her mind?

We pass quickly, as though
walking away moves us beyond it.
Still pretending distance makes
anything remote, I look back
and see their turned eyes following,
lips pulled down as if by hooks.

Chinese Camp, California

A rich vein of hating,

a pen to keep them working in

until they dropped,

a guidebook to lead me through then out to here,

where the prospect is only broader,

the vein not yet exhausted,

history the pen

big enough to enclose all of us—

yellow by yellow

me by them.

L'Autre

It must be the loveliest of places:

Grey mist forms on the window

passing such singleness

to a place.

Not to spoil by stopping.

Simply a choice.

You'll travel

until you find a bus

to come home to.

The Word

"Those who live by the word
Will die listening,"

—Delmore Schwartz

A simple recognition
instructs those who live
by the word.

To have ears grained by
the mind's listening
is to live in a well.

Words to plunk like pennies
into always drinking water.
I hear. I hear, echoes
louder than the sound
of senses –

recreate the mind's music
like deaf mutes
singing.

The Ass

Wistful, he speaks of hope

to outstride his despair

and separates a lie of one

without the other

as strict proportion of

flesh to bone

to exist always

a pace behind,

he cannot face it.

Photo Album

It's like peering

into a dark cave

and discovering

it has been abandoned

even by mystery.

Imagination moves

each foot backwards,

trailing a reticent past

where memory hangs

like a sleeping bat.

A Fable

Once, it must have been news
to somebody: the Woman who
married the Dog.

And this was nothing obscene,
like the hiking of skirts
and crawling backwards
on hands and knees,
but a Woman's understanding
of the old cur's wants.

She made the bed in which
he buried his bone,
proved an alternative
to his fleas, and was
as lovely as a Tree.
And so they lived.
The Woman imperative
as Pleasure, the Dog giving
gradually into Hope.

Which to a Dog is an unknown premise,

though to a Man, a common place.

Tail to wag the Dog.

The Fool

The old man fingering the magazines

given him.

Tense laughter and pieces of cake

falling from his mouth.

And a hand stretched

like intention

over the photograph. Looks

to see across the page –

no woman,

no use.

Marginal Notes From a Los Alamos Journal

For J. Robert Oppenheimer

We are told that a demonstration is not sufficient,
and we believe it.

Too much has been invested for us to recover from a fall now. After
all, science teaches that a man broken down into his elements is
hardly worth recycling.

Somewhere, the Creator sits at home ill at ease and unsure,
stamping out the first cigarette
because already he sees a spot on his lung.

Here we have witnessed pure creation. Our eyes have the pallor of
bones bleached clean by unrelenting sun.
But we know too that elsewhere this desert's heat can make the
blood boil.

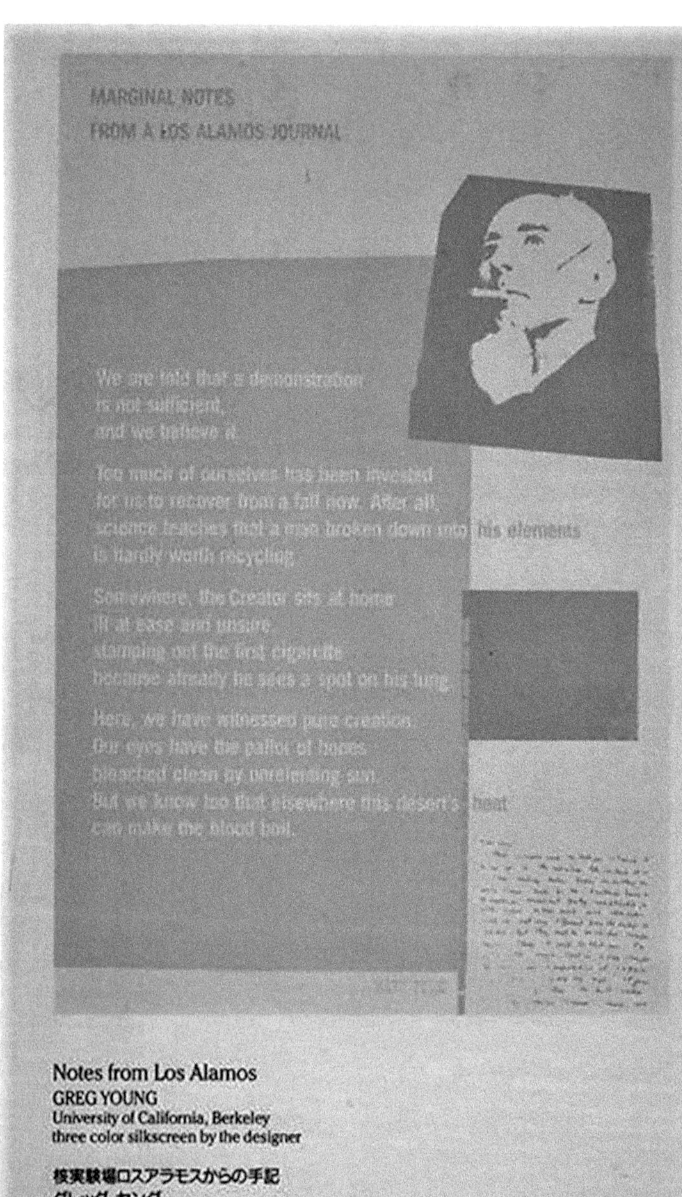

Notes from Los Alamos
GREG YOUNG
University of California, Berkeley
three color silkscreen by the designer

検索験場ロスアラモスからの手記
グレッグ ヤング

Exhibition of my poem, "Marginal Notes from a Los Alamos Journal", is at the Hiroshima Museum of Art. Graphic artist Greg Young incorporated a facsimile of J. Robert Oppenheimer's handwritten notes about testing the atomic bomb, an iconic photo of him smoking a cigarette together with a washed-out desert scene. The poster's colors are purposely faded as if exposed to a high burning light. The poster received several national awards and toured several major U.S. art galleries before being chosen for display in Hiroshima, Japan.

Photograph

She is young, slender, and almost pretty.

And her pose—if that is what it was—displays

a grace normally associated with less girlish frames. One hand

holds a few strands of hair, and nearby,

the other grasps a large comb placed almost in her lap. She is

wearing a paisley dress; the zipper undone,

it hangs loosely around her shoulders, and her face is turned toward

something beyond the photo's border. Who she is,

what she meant, the memory I thought to preserve, have all left me.

I know only that I was with her

in a room years ago, and that the sun filtering

into that room faded instantly upon striking the floor.

Only film exposed to that light for a brief instant of time has kept

her, relieved of sense,

of any purpose but of being there. Intent in that time but looking

away.

Polygraph

"The instruments of darkness tell us truths, Win us with honest trifles, to betray's

In deepest consequence."

—Macbeth

Things were clearer the first time they strapped you in, "fluttered"
you, as they call it.
Your motives to conceal were so pure that each response
only made the operator smile.

With practice you grew more cunning:
every answer given was like a plant
whose sole purpose was to retreat underground into a seed.

From the man behind the machine, you learned to cultivate
plausible explanations
from grains so scrupulous and small.

These occasional chats amuse you now
as you zigzag an unseen and inaccessible route. When you ask for
a glass of water,

perhaps he believes you're only thirsty,

and that may be true, but so are a hundred other things.

Runaway

She said it was always to be fearful
of losing the way. That the path
might end long before you called it quits.
It was like that when your parents died,
or with your first girl. When all your
chances were used by someone else.

Now twenty years later you still sleep
on the floor, fearing the unmade bed
will give you away. When you leave
for the last time, be certain the
figure watching you from the overpass
cannot see the expression on your face,
lest she believe that regret has nothing
to do with love, that nothing's left to chance
now that there's everything to lose.

Excerpts from a California Childhood

I had just been in the neighborhood for a few weeks and already found myself invited to a birthday party for a boy who lived down the street. I barely knew him, having spoken to him only briefly during one of my patrols around the block in an effort to make friends. I suppose his mother had invited me as a courtesy. Still, I was happy enough at the prospect of meeting some other kids that I overcame my shyness and asked my mother to buy something special to impress him.

The following Sunday my father dropped me off in front of the Sacramento Racquet Club. Since it was a swimming party, I was dressed only in my trunks and rubble sandals. I had a large bath towel slung around my neck and clutched the quarter my mom had given me for admission. And, of course, I had Doug's birthday gift, a plastic B-52 bomber, which I would have loved to have kept for myself.

There were about fifteen of us, all boys, all around eight years old. As we began filing through the turnstile, we all because excited and rowdy at the prospect of Doug's party. One of the boys at the head of the line shouted "Geronimo!" and flung himself forward as he passed the turnstile, pretending to parachute out of the Clubhouse doorway. This set off a chain reaction as each kid deposited his quarter and leapt with varying degrees of proficiency across the entrance.

When it was my turn, however, the man at the counter stopped me. I was afraid that I didn't have enough money, but that wasn't the problem. He pointed to a sign above the chalkboard behind him. "The Racquet Club does no admit Negroes, Mexicans or Orientals in our pool."

I didn't understand. Everyone could swim at my old neighborhood pool in South Side Park. The man explained that it was the rule and returned my quarter. Although confused at first, this statement seemed to satisfy the rest of the kids. They look at me if deciding whether I had done something wrong. I grew hot and ref-faced, and I felt vaguely ashamed. I left the line and stood by the doorway, too embarrassed to speak to anyone.

After a while I left and walked across the club's parking lot to the chain link fence that surrounded the swimming pool. I saw the other children splashing about in the shallow end. When they saw me standing there, some would come up and shyly speak to me. But it was a hot afternoon and they soon forgot about me. I stood there all afternoon, sweat dripping down my face as I watched them doing cannon balls and being scolded by the lifeguard. I remember waving to Doug to get his attention. I motioned to the wrapped birthday gift I was still carrying and tossed it over the fence. Then I walked home, too ashamed to call for a ride.

I didn't want my parents to know what had happened. When I reached my house I sneaked into the backyard and hosed myself down with water. As I entered the house, my mom asked, "Did you have a good time?" You've been gone so long, and you're so red"

"It was lots of fun," I said. But my back got sunburned when I was playing out of the pool." She looked at me but didn't say anything. Later I heard her tell my father that I couldn't have gone swimming. My trunks didn't smell of chlorine.

* * *

My mother, one of three children, grew up in genteel poverty in prewar San Francisco. Her mother was a widow who spoke only a few words of English and who provided for her family by working as a domestic. My father was raised in Sacramento. His father was a humorless authoritarian figure who forced him to study English, Japanese, Latin, German and music—believing that to be the standard extracurricular regimen for an American youngster.

One of my father's duties was to care for his invalid mother, whose health had been deteriorating since she arrived in this country and who was becoming increasing withdrawn. Refined, artistic and highly educated for a Japanese woman of that period, she found her proscribed life in the coarse and racist America of the 1920s and 1920s unbearable. She died a victim of rudeness which is a disease as much as any physical ailment.

* * *

Like most Japanese American, my parents suffered from the national hysteria of the Second World War. My father especially. An undergraduate at the University of Oregon, he had just been awarded a law scholarship when Pearl Harbor was bombed. He was booted out of college six days later and found himself in the Tule Lake relocation camp within a month. It was there that he met my mother.

After the war, the anti-Japanese sentiment in California was too strong for my parents to return. There followed another several years of relocation—until they gingerly returned to the West Coast. They moved into my father's old house in South Side Park. In the next ten years, the once tranquil neighborhood was transformed by housing developments, an influx of the unemployable and a rising crime rate. One Sunday morning my mother saw one of tenants next store wearing a sweater that belonged to my sister. Tired of having clothing stolen off the drying line from our backyard, my mother confronted the neighbor and asked for the sweater. The women, more than twice the size of my mother, slugged her powerfully in her stomach. We moved again.

In our new house, in an old, glass-paneled mahogany bookcase that belonged to my grandfather, were the leather bound law books my father received as the traditional component of his scholarship. They were musty, unused and long out of date. My father never referred to them, and he never threw them out.

* * *

My first day at my new elementary school made a huge difference ten miles from South Side Park could make. My clothes, a pressed flannel shirt, heavy corduroy pants and study black-soled shoes, were not only inappropriate but laughable. Moreover, my

27

behavior was all wrong. I was gregarious in the face of my classmates' lack of enthusiasm: too eager to please while they stood off in disdainful self-assurance.

But it wasn't all appearances. They were more well-to-do children, unaccustomed to hand-me-down clothing and the necessity of packing a bag lunch to school, making sure to keep the sack clean so it could be used through the week. They belonged to tennis clubs and some even went horseback riding. Their families went skiing in the winter time (a "rich man's sport", my father scoffed.) They went to a barbershop to get their haircuts. I spent a miserable week being ridiculed when I stupidly confided to a classmate that my father cut my hair at home.

The most prominent status symbol was a bicycle. The children at Alice Birney (named after the founder of the P.T.A.) Elementary School rode magnificent ones, brand new Schwinns with headlights, mirror and shiny chrome hand brakes. They didn't inherit third hand rusting hulks with bear metal seats and comically miniature 13" inch wheels. I was so embarrassed about my bike that I hid it each morning in a grassy field near the school and walked the remaining distance. One day my grandmother discovered it barely concealed among the weeds and angrily warned me that someone might steal it. Of course no one ever did.

* * *

Since both my parents worked—another rarity among the neighborhood—the burden of raising me fell to my maternal grandmother. From the time I was born to my early adolescence—with the exception of a few unhappy years when she was sent to live with my uncle as part of the burden sharing—I was under her care.

In our new neighborhood my grandmother's entire world consisted of the rooms in our house and the backyard. Occasionally she would venture out on walks around the block. He inability to speak English and her slow, bent shuffle was highly amusing to the children in the neighborhood who sometimes followed her on these jaunts, mimicking her duck-like gait.

My most vivid memory of her was when I was ten years old, during one of my father's extravagant Christmas parties. Every year he hosted a sumptuous banquet for his post office colleagues and their wives. My mother and grandmother worked for days beforehand to prepare the exotic Japanese food in quantities that seemed to grow each year. Lavish food and ample supplies of liquor made the parties famous, and invitations were avidly sought.

The guests at these parties were the people whose acceptance was important to my father. So my brothers and sister and I preened ourselves for their inspection, unobtrusively cleaned up their spilled drinks, and pretended to be amused by their loud and often vulgar remarks.

The din throughout the house increased as more and more guests arrived. My mother and sister darted from one person to the next with plates piled high with food; one of my brothers was sent out to the store for more ice, while another freshened drinks held by unsteady hands, anonymous hands. My task was to collect coats and wraps from the guests and place them in one of the bedrooms for safekeeping.

As I opened the door to my sister's room, the light poured in from the hall and I saw a small figure silhouetted against the wall. It was my grandmother. She was sitting erect on one of the twin beds in the room she shared with my sister. On each side of her were mountainous piles of neatly folded coats. She was an embarrassment to my father, a discordant note in his carefully orchestrated harmony of assimilation. Although she was largely responsible for the exquisite feast being gobbled up outside, she sat in the dark, hidden, unacknowledged and very still.

The image of my grandmother shrouded in the darkness, silent and unobserved, is among my most intense childhood memories. It became a touchstone representing that day I was not admitted to the Sacramento Racquet Club. For the first time in my life I had felt misplaced. A sense of place, of belonging somewhere, vanished while I stood looking longing through a high, chain fence. It was an ironic parody of my parents' own wartime experience. Perhaps it was an inevitable lesson of time, hurried along by an introduction to the world outside. I would never again feel so unreservedly happy or so at home.

Awarded First Prize for Nonfiction writing in Bumbershoot Arts Festival. Published in Ergo! and later made part of the Seattle Public Schools curriculum.

Salt

"What a beautiful faith it is to expect the tide pools to replenish the sea every night."

—From a Japanese fable

It's no accident we crawled out of the sea.
Everything derives from its bitterness—
tears, sweat, semen.

Tonight in a voice raw with salt, you tell me your father is dying,
his cells being eaten by a disease we name for the crab.

Now you must understand death from a bottle washed up on a shore
sent out to anyone.

As sons we see our fathers as oceans whose depths remain
unknowable
and in whose currents we remain forever
puny and partially derived.

Tonight the heart's dark current recedes into the pallid cupped
hands of the moon,

emptying us of a child's faith
that all tides are eternal.

And if we can't believe in legends
that tell of oceans nightly restored by vapor,
we are still grateful for the mere cycle
of blood flowing back and forth,
as between tide pool and sea
no less great in its passing.

Double Vision

For Sue

Because you seek order above all else,
don't be surprised you'd abandon it so quickly
for what is staring back through such soft
animal eyes, black and lovely,
fulfilling themselves with shyness
like those of a deer approaching
your proffered hand, trusting its own speed
and your gentleness.

Anyway, that's how you imagine it,
wanting to feel her breath on your skin.
So you empty your pockets like a boy,
searching for the right combination

of hidden treats to feed the hunger
you share by instinct.

Like a perfect hunter gone soft,
you've become sentimental about
foragers, exalting in this one's smooth gait
and indiscriminate sensual appetites.

Outside of that awkward woman you see
into is a sly child whose eyes grin wildly,
pretending not to notice you looking
as she romps in your loving
attention as though into a pile of
leaves,
already forgiven for her wanton undoing.

Revelation

One morning you find a note
tacked to your door
and the house empty,
or awake to discover the phone
cradled in your lap,
the bad news over hours ago.

This is when you make the tea
strong and hot, spend the extra time
to cook the eggs just the way you like.
For some, the first sign is a noise
behind them, and no time,
no time at all.

Dying Arts

For Avi, Killed in Lebanon

Long distance is expensive,

so the messages were short.

First the call from the consulate,

then confirmation by telegram:

the best Jew in the service

has bought the kibbutz.

Few here let out war whoops.

It was bound to happen

had you stayed and not defected.

You were finally overtaken

by the same choices we made years ago,

when a dutiful and pretentious bastard

could see the road going on forever.

In Cairo, you pointed to a wash of stars

and marveled at how people could be duped

into believing in them long after

they had grown cold and dead,

light taking so long to reach us.

Our business was like that—to keep

the morons guessing, you said.

 Death has lost its random aspects,

and there is nothing more unprofessional

than faith. Still, Avrum, my beloved

old friend, sometimes pretense is the light that fills the enormity of

the sky.

```
4-0324758160 06/09/82 ICS IPMMTZZ CSP OAKB
 2023511152 MGM TDMT WASHINGTON DC 18 06-09 0155P EST


MARK OSAKI
PO BOX 9024
BERKELEY CA 94709



AVI'S DEATH CONFIRMED. LEBANON LAST WEEK. AM VERY SORRY
  KALEV

13:55 EST

MGMCOMP MGM
```

Amnesiac

For a while I too was haunted by
memories of your frightened faces
as we hovered nearby, shooting
warning tracers above your heads.
It was amazing—you thought waving
American flags would save you.

We had other rooftops to fly to.
Coming back from the last one,
we saw the fire you had set as a beacon.
We couldn't help it. We laughed.

The cries and curses you threw up
into that sky were instantly
drowned out and chopped up
by bladed arks already flying away.

I am among my own now, who do not
worship stones or rivers or impute
to them a memory of any kind.
What does not perish here by forgetting

survives only in the occasional bad dream.

We wake up each morning to a new history.
We don't know if we remember.

Turista

From the verandah I watch the jetsam
of another election
flash before me like gunfire.
Perhaps out of guilt, I promise myself
a sticky slice of fried banana for everybody
that is crumpled against the blackened wall
in the courtyard below.

Back home, a man my age is voting
for the first time. Here a sentry
is positioned on every rooftop
to remind the electorate who won.
I would wave, but they have seen enough
of my hands moving under the skirts
of this inherited country.

Already I am thinking of Paris, my reward.
I take another warm section of fruit
and compose my next cable:
Situation improving. Stop. They're using
our rifles.

Preserve

This is the playground
of the enemy's youth:
upturned graves and craters
to swim in when it rains.
Small children shake skulls
like rattles,
while older ones carve rifles
out of bone,
making what use of the time
given them.

Family Reunion

It was always worse
just before we disembarked,
while the Hueys hovered,
insolently slapping the air.

Pointing to me, someone shouted,
Throw him out first,
one look and the gooks
will think we're friendly.

That's right, fellas,
the CO laughed,
this boy has kin
out there.

It amused me too
to imagine someone hiding below us in the grass
with my photo in his wallet.

It was a joke
to be shared

with everyone

we killed.

Gun Song

We have become accustomed to taking one to bed

like a nightmare

kept under the pillow

for just those times

persuasion must be fatal,

as when we huddled

in fear and anger,

threatening the

 awaited intruder,

our mouths a ragged

ache of holes

against the familiar

impact.

Ghost Story

Sometimes while passing a playground,
you'll see a child so like my mother
you believe for the length of a pang
it's me.

You can't understand I'm not a child
anymore, that I have, like you,
grown older.

If there is joy in even the smallest
secret, then I was your greatest,
never to be shared because there was
no other you loved.

But now I am asking you to see
that even the dead change
with time.

There are no memories of me to forget,
only that I was the beginning
of a past you keep forcing
into the future.

I'm too big to be carried, even by a father,

and you were never as strong as you pretended to be.

South of the Border

When they uncover what you buried here,
how will you explain an order carried out
in heat and simple frustration?

Your good intentions evaporated
in every seething village until, like fever,
you broke.

Surprising how a body warms
to oppressive surroundings.
Things rot quickly in the tropics.

This, too, you can blame on the climate.

An Old Dance Favor

Throughout the neon-lit ward,
braces thunder to the music
no one can hear.
The wooden ribs of the floor
are splitting under the weight
of so much metal.

An attendant smiles at me
and shouts, It's therapy!
He motions to a chair atop which my friend is propped, his torso
swaying in time with the stumbling shapes
dancing on stumps.

Silver Star

Patriotism is nothing more than the memory of the good things we ate as children.

Because you are among the lucky,

you have been chosen to escort

this oblong container on the long journey home.

Beneath its star-spangled wrapper

is one of a thousand government-issue Twinkies,

so called because it contains a body bag

or "cream filling."

Impaled on a frosting of stars is another

solitary gold pentagram,

a decoration for pacifying a piece of Asia

for twenty minutes.

Whatever he died for—this guy over whom you

rest your boot—will be solemnly misunderstood

in the ceremony he is flying so far to attend.

But you, the fortunate living,

are not thinking about that.

Your stomach rumbles in unison

with the plane's engines as you dream

of hamburgers, fries, and pizza.

When the tires scorch the runway's apron,
your last unconscious thought is of something
burning on a neighborhood grill.

The cargo bay opens; the hot afternoon air
is heavy, sticky, and sweet.
You walk erect in blinking silence,
but soon you are leaping in rewarded joy
through golden arches of childhood memories,
an affirmation of country, a welcoming home.

Canticle

For love to recognize the end
-- if there is any final meeting –
It is on its own conditions.
Not a change of terms,
Only a changed relation"
You move and are gone,
I move and remain.
A face unregarded (then and now)
Surrenders all its seeming
To another darkness or
To another light, this
Is what emptiness is for.

The same haunts will not come again.
Time will flow back from
A common past, gentled, as if
No parting stretched between us, and
Ask pardon for how selfhood began
With a walking away, and love proven
In a letting go.

What we began is now its own—
So long hidden, a divided secret,
And a grief less lonely
For what love, unwished, was once.

Tradecraft

Icon

Once, in a great while,

you will see a sign

and invest in it everything

out of simple faith

it is meant for you.

You will surrender

all you've been taught

to the purity of its direction

and stand perfectly still,

knowing nothing more is beyond it.

This is how they will find you:

unable to break away, peering steadfast from the threshold,

starved by certainty,

blessed forever and unobserved.

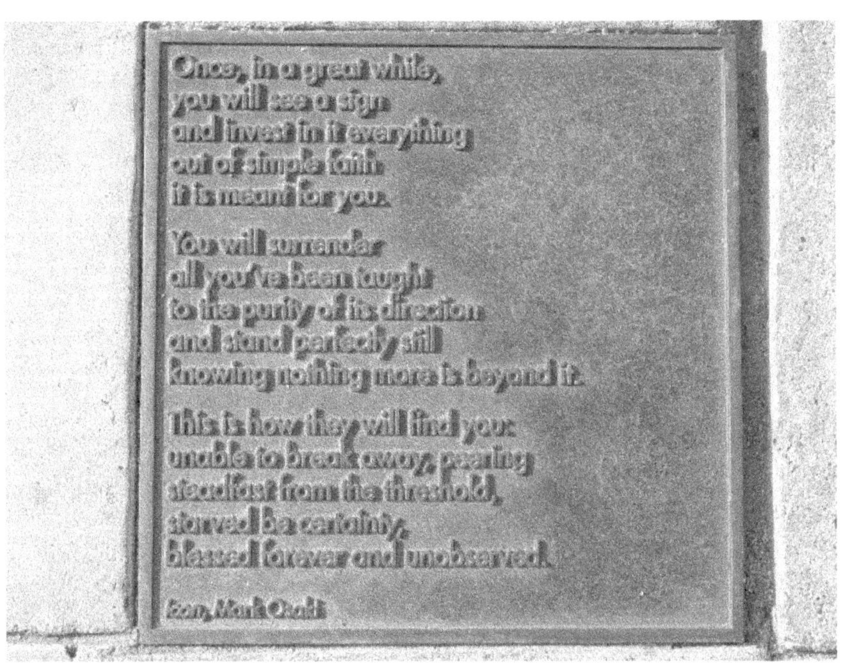

SF Art Commission Historic Signage Program Plaque on Embarcadero

Border Exchange

Of course she's a spy.
A secret for each kiss
is fair trade
when betrayal is only
the last concession.

No matter what
you'd rather believe,
her face moves lovingly
in your lap, the soft
old hotel bed is adequate,
and what you whisper
in her ear is true
enough.

Cachet

Remember it is a brief power.
You possess it
over objections.

Feel its cold heft,
the way it fits
your hand, fills it.

What do you want?
someone asks.
Just point.

Contentment

None of our warnings sank in.
He was already celebrating
 the reunion at the border, his
daughter's first ballet lessons,
the promise of the other side.

We've all dreamed of that crossing:
a river to erase our tracks, the welcome
in the clearing just ahead, the guide
who becomes our one love.
Years spent accustomed to others
failing have brought us quiet relief
in not making the effort.

Days later we followed his trial
in the papers and made cruel jokes
about the clothesline he had carried,
not half what he would have needed.
After the rains, the only sign left
was a girl's weathered shoe
still caught in the wire.

Elsewhere, perhaps it makes sense
to have a destination worth so much risk.

Possible even to make good an escape
using a rope so short it seems fit
only for a hanging.

Ambush

Always it's the suddenness of attack
that makes defense impossible.
The loon kicked up from nowhere
who pirouettes before you,
seizing by chance your lapels
to help slow her mad dance.

All my family, she gasps,
dead. Killed in the Balkans!
You don't know history!
You know nothing!
Each accusation is a hard
bony bruise in my chest.

Had I strength,
I might pry her off me,
overturn the old refugee
like a cart along the road.
But it is she who breaks away,
despising my tolerance,
burdening her back again

with the furtive pain

she had escaped with
so long ago.

I might have known.
Her kind usually strike
on open ground, when you're tired,
pecked at by small hurts,
leaving work on a hot afternoon,
with only home
to keep you marching.

Jamaica

It was when you said my breath
had become salty that we laughed,
tongues exhausted from the last tidal swell,
and saw the whole island still quavering
under the moon's stiffened light.

I am become your seal, you said,
grinning. A pure obsession nailed
to tissue and fin as water hammered
in waves by shaken spray, lapping
wetness on an emerging skin.

Your belly full of headless fish,
the foam glistening on your lips,
your face diving into me so cold and
lovely to touch, a flat black mammal
swimming into meat.

Such a Lovely Dress

For Sue Toigo

Let's pretend that fulfillment
is just another dress
that I can compliment.
Easy discretion that allows
no shielding of eyes
or the delicate harm
of a lingering afterthought.

We are lucky to have such distractions
to keep us faithful to necessity.
Chances narrow with experience,
and what is hope but proof of pain
after all. Better to be understood
than loved, you said.

Better a dance of manners
that claims nothing
and wastes each momentary promise
with playful approval,
as though you've saved your whole life
for some new dress.

You'll Miss Me When I'm Gone

There was never an intelligent design at work
to stave off a sky so dark as this:
Hoards of buzzing of insects so vast,
gnawing holes through the humid air;
masters of an inheritance unchallenged
by anything so pitifully unnoticed
as a box of bones and the solitary
human imprint on the ground below
turned to stone, so long,
so long ago
leaving nothing to wonder.

And you, likewise
not young or unbroken enough
for innocence,
can smile back in purposeless agreement
that as we understand
we too love.

Unspoken Correspondence

All night I dreamed of you
trying to free a child's name
hooked deeply in your throat,
your gasping mouth a dark hole
emptied of everything
but a single word.

In a place already fluent with pain,
you have the whisper of a chance
stuck with the son,
the undying echo
you can't pronounce.

If I say nothing,
you will understand
how sorry the tongue is
concerning these things,
how tied to its roots
is grief.

Going Quietly

Sometimes it begins with a job
you really hate,
a place where the universe shrinks
to the size of one hard tongue.

Already it's difficult to recall
when failure meant anything
but being late.

The time is past for taking yourself
seriously: you like your boss,
you're saving for a car,
only little things upset you now.

Listening to your own voice
grow dim,
you swear you were deaf to it.

Tradecraft

The first lesson is as simple
as the looking glass.
A deception you read from left to right.
Reflection tells you
who is being taken in.

Gradually you'll recognize
every hoax by its face,
like the image you now confront
and the steel trap
that frames it.

Best Evidence

Mentor

In this version Odysseus was just too busy,

so his son went instead,

a little disgusted at how comfortable

the old man had become.

And it was fun living by his wits,

wryly observing the passing scene

with the smugness of all travelers, but after ten years even Troy

made him think of dust and ashes.

So when the world had finally shrunk

to his satisfaction,

he returned to discover the city free of plots,

his mother still mistress of the house,

and there on his table

the book he had always wanted to read,

with some passages underlined

by his father.

The Crisis

As I sit writing this,

I am pretending you are

sitting on my lap and

that I've slipped into you,

so tired, so easy.

Or, is it to be another way:

on all fours, back broken

as a man to learn

when any lover

can be a chair.

Legacy

Maybe you did some good,
keeping company with her
absent children, old TV
shows, and silence.

Tough, you thought, though
the face in the car's mirror
never hardened during
the numbing ride back.

I know you'll miss
the nice drive up, she'd
said at last. Grateful
to have given you something.

Juba Luke

He is beloved but cannot speak
or feel the heat until it burns his skin
and the sores open and the commotion begins.
Even now, he remains motionless for hours
inside his warm and humid room,
a long tongue lolling over his scaly lip
in anticipation of the leafy collards
Mama is lovingly growing in the garden.
The soft, clean folds of his belly
sag upon the bare mattress,
his rear legs roped to the floor,
not minding, not minding at all.

Looking for Dover Beach

It was always to be searching
over the rim of the coffee cup
into eyes that returned nothing.

Constancy seemed mere habit now.
The dark had gentler hands,
impeccable and impersonal.

Time had dignified the hurts
like a scream muffled through layers
of neatly laundered cloth.

But despite the sense things made,
sometimes she hears the roar of it,
the beautiful crashing down

of an empty building.

νησί των γατών (Isle of Cats)

For Cindy Kawahata

The Greeks were right;

it is a place of darkness,

so heavy with mist that even Charon

could not steer a path to your destination.

Where is the promised guide?

Or is that the myth they tell us

so we won't fear being unbearably alone?

Everything we love assumes

a distinct shape that we cannot see

until it approaches us on cat paws, unafraid.

That was life then.

Now, you feel a familiar brushing against your leg,

and bend to touch the head purring softly

in this eternal night.

Killer

We are born into a uniform of skin

that limits the authority

of our helplessness.

Sooner or later

years of giving ground,

for those who have practiced endlessly

to stare straight ahead

in smoldering silence,

is enough

to reach for concealed justice

and trigger a final reckoning.

Destinations

For Jenny Smagala Luciano

It was never meant to be a practical guide,

if you are both blessed and cursed

to live from one surprise to the next.

In truth, you prefer the out-of-the-way places

to the paved land bridge across

what is always visible and taken for granted.

The unseen dots eventually connect

and make one wary of hope:

the lump that should not be there

or the hesitant look that comes too late.

Children have taught you to accept

gratitude over happiness,

as you faithfully follow the heart's traceable map

of far dreams leading ever away

but always returning home.

Homecoming

Nothing has ever kept me home.
Somehow every train or bus
has always departed without regret.
Going becomes the habit of all travelers,
and I've been away too long
for the scenery to remind me
that there was after all
a point of departure.

This is not to say I believe
your waving hand means anything
more than we think it does.
Only a man who is likewise uncertain
of returning can see the packed suitcases
in your eyes, the smile in need of assurance
arriving right on schedule to greet me,
as though you had been waiting all along.

Snow

Saigon

The photograph is badly smudged,
most of the girls are lost forever,
with the missing half torn away
years ago.
Their poses would have been what
you'd expect: a lineup before
the orphanage wall, the starched
jumpers, the disposing faces of
the nuns; except for the lone girl
at the end, not holding anyone's hand.
Unsmiling, her eyes look
fitfully into yours.
Below her, someone has written,
Antoinette-Snow
Hors le péché original.

Paris

In the embassy garden, she stared at you
like a girl cornered by passion
for the first time, then smiled,

certain.

All winter she became the likeness

you had always believed in.

That last night you flew across

the Channel and watched the moon

light her face, her white camisole,

like a final memory.

Saigon

It was as though you had completed

a nightmare begun long ago

by finding the picture's vanished half:

the row of girls aren't even

looking at the camera.

They are turned toward her, each

holds the hand of the other.

Last in this succession, a nun, who

reaches for a frightened girl's arm.

McLean, Virginia

From a file you take a smudged,

 torn photo of a girl so beautiful

it is as if she came into the world

without parents.
More than a lifetime has passed
since she was pulled back into
that atavistic light.
Then, too, a shutter closed
and left you this: a past

already developing into your future,
a contrast of black and white,
gray resemblances,
and love flattened paper-thin.

Beginning's End (Tule Lake, California 1942)

In the photo my mother is twenty years old.

She is leaning against the railing

of a shoddily built prison barrack

wondering if the climate

could get any more hostile.

She is very pretty;

her lush black curls fall around her face,

she is wearing her best flowered cotton skirt,

and her slender legs disappear like stilts

into bobby sox and saddle shoes.

She thinks this must be punishment

for some unfathomable karmic sin:

that all your life can be confined

into two suitcases and relocated

across a remote California desert.

Yet she is smiling past the camera's static eye,

knowing how very much will depend

on the shadowed figure in the distance

with a hand already waving in recognition;

or perhaps making a fist.

Old Man Thinking of Small Breasts

Forty years from now,
will there be another man
lost in an orchard that
has grown up around him?

To have known him all his life
and have it come to this:
watching him covet the small
roundish fruit of the trees.

His dry lips cracking all the while.
The wrinkled hands holding the
speckled skin, feeling its suppleness.
The mind daydreaming, grasping at
anything but firm. Thinking hard
hurts the teeth.

About the Author

Mark S. Osaki was born in Sacramento, California. He attended the University of California, Berkeley as an Alumni Scholar and went on to do graduate work in International Relations and Security Studies.

His work has appeared in various journals and anthologies, including: *The Georgia Review*, *Carrying the Darkness—The Poetry of the Vietnam War* (Avon, Texas Tech University Press), *South Carolina Review, Men of Our Time—An Anthology of Male Poetry in Contemporary America* (University of Georgia Press), *Breaking Silence—An Anthology of Contemporary Asian American Poets* (Greenfield Review Press), *Onset Review and Báo Giấy— Vietnamese Poetry*.

Osaki has received awards for his poetry from the Academy of American Poets, University of California at Berkeley, San Francisco Arts Commission, Seattle Arts Council and the National Endowment for the Arts.

https://www.amazon.com/author/markosaki